CLOCKS
TELL
THE TIME

ALMA KEHOE RECK

ILLUSTRATIONS BY
JANINA DOMANSKA

CHARLES SCRIBNER'S SONS, NEW YORK

To Marjorie Rebecca Reck, my daughter

The author expresses appreciation for the kind assistance of Mr. ORVILLE R. HAGANS, owner of Clock Manor Museum, Denver, Colorado.

Grateful acknowledgment is made to the following for permission to use adaptations of photographs and pictures:

THE METROPOLITAN MUSEUM OF ART, Dick Fund 1934 for detail from A Clockmaker's Work Shop by Johannes Stradanus

THE PIERPONT MORGAN LIBRARY for M 429 *Beatus of Liebana* (Bell Tower)

The editors of *A History of Technology*, volume III, and the Clarendon Press, Oxford, for cock from original Strasbourg Clock

THE CLOCK MANOR MUSEUM, Denver, Colorado for Elephant Clock (1700)

THE NATIONAL COMPANY, Malden, Mass. for adaptation from photograph of Atomichron

CONTENTS

H-4005

WE NEED CLOCKS

Time-telling brings order and rhythm to living, and clocks tell the time. Life in our busy, modern world would be very confusing without clocks.

Even in ancient times man saw the need for a time-keeper. Where there is a great need, people usually try to do something about it. The clock was not "invented" by any one man. People all around the world tried to fill the need for a time-keeper in different ways.

Through the years many ways of telling time came into use. There were shadow clocks and sundials, water clocks and sandglasses, bell clocks and candle clocks, tower and steeple clocks, grandfather clocks and shelf clocks. Many were in use at the same time.

For centuries clocks were made one at a time by hand. They were not very accurate, but more of an expensive ornament. They were found only in the palaces of kings and the homes of very wealthy people.

Today clocks are made by the thousand in modern factories. Families may have several clocks in their houses.

SHADOW CLOCKS

The sun was primitive man's first time-piece. These early people lived outdoors or in caves. For them life was simple. Their food came from wild game in the forest, nuts and berries from the fields, and fish from the streams. They did not need to know the *exact* time as we do today.

Prehistoric man noticed that the sun seemed to "rise" out of the earth or sky. Then it was time to get up. When the sun "set" and darkness came, it was time to go to sleep. Primitive man did not know, as we do today, that the earth turns on its axis as it goes around the sun.

Prehistoric man noticed that the sun cast shadows. He noticed that the shadows changed in size and shape during the day. When he went out to hunt he may have pointed to a shadow cast by a tree, or perhaps a stone or a cliff. He may have said that he would return when the shadow reached a certain place. Perhaps he placed a stick in the ground so that the shadow would be sharper.

Man also noticed that the moon had a strange way of changing shape. Sometimes the moon looked like a golden

6

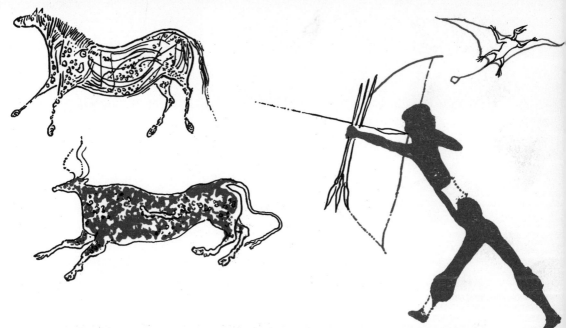

ball. Sometimes it looked like a half circle. At other times
it was a crescent, and sometimes it did not appear at all.
These changes happened over and over again, and always
in the same way. Man used the moon as a time-piece
when he arranged to meet a friend at a certain place "next
full moon."

The years went by. People no longer lived in caves.
They lived in houses of stone, wood, or bricks baked in
the sunshine. They divided the time roughly into seasons
by the budding of trees and plants, the falling of leaves,
the coming of the dry or rainy seasons, the migrations of
birds, and other signs of nature.

They began to raise crops. They had a time for planting,
a time for growing, and a time for harvest.

At this time the farmer may have improved his shadow
clock by placing stones to mark the changing positions
of the shadow cast by the sun; though we do not really
know that he did so.

Reconstruction of the gate of Babylon

Early Assyrian Astronomers

TELLING TIME BY THE STARS

The people began to move together to form villages and towns. Some lived in well-built cities of brick and stone. One of these cities was called Babylon. Here lived a group of wise men who liked to observe the sun, moon, and stars.

These men were *astronomers*. Although they had no telescopes and only the most primitive scientific instruments, they discovered many things about the stars and planets. They noticed that the Pole Star was a "fixed" star. Other groups of stars seemed to change position.

These Babylonian astronomers and other ancient astronomers imagined a belt around the sky which we still call the Zodiac. They divided this belt into twelve sections, each named for a certain group of stars. The Greeks gave us the word Zodiac which means "circle of animals." Most of the signs of the Zodiac are animals.

Modern astronomers with their understanding of science and mathematics and the use of improved instruments can tell almost the exact time by the stars.

SUNDIALS

As the years passed, men learned more about astronomy and science. They began to learn trades. Some became weavers and carpenters. Others were potters and stonemasons. Some people opened stores to supply the needs of others. A more accurate timepiece was needed.

The idea of the sundial may have grown out of the stick-and-shadow clock. It is one of the oldest time-telling devices in the world. Instead of the stick, an upright piece called the *gnomon* was used. *Gnomon* is a Greek word meaning "one who knows." The gnomon was placed on a plate or dial. The sun cast the shadow of the gnomon on different parts of the dial as the earth turned on its axis. The word dial comes from the Latin and means *day*.

Later men found that the time could be told more accurately by pointing the gnomon toward the North Pole. The dial was divided into quarters with the dividing line running toward the points of the compass: North, South, East, and West. Still later the dial was divided into hours.

10

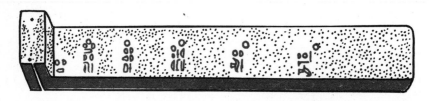

Old Egyptian sundial

The sundial could not tell time on cloudy or rainy days. It could not tell time at night. But for hundreds of years, it was the only clock that many people had.

There were many interesting kinds of sundials.

The largest sundial in the world is said to be the one at Jaiphur, India. Its gnomon is 147 feet long, and it stands 90 feet high.

Some sundials were made so small they could be carried in the pocket. George Washington, our first president, owned one of these and used it to tell the time on sunny days.

Today sundials are still used as garden ornaments. Some of them are marked with the words, "I count only the hours that shine."

11

Sundial
on Cathedral at Chartres

Garden sundial

WATER CLOCKS

In those ancient times there was little or no communication between cities and countries. People in different parts of the world learned to tell time in different ways.

No one knows who first used the water clock. It may have been used in some places before the sundial. This way of telling time was used in China, Egypt, Arabia, Rome, Greece, and through Europe for many, many years. The Greeks called their water clock a *clepsydra*, which means "thief of water."

Old Egyptian waterclock

The simplest of water clocks was an earthen bowl marked with rings inside. This had a small hole in the bottom. The bowl was filled with water to a certain mark, and it would empty at a fairly even rate. This water clock was used in Greece and Rome to time the length of speeches.

In India another form of water clock was used. An empty bowl with a small hole in the bottom was placed in a larger vessel of water. Time was measured by the length of time it took the smaller vessel to fill with water and sink. Then the clock-tender would recover the smaller bowl, empty it, and repeat the process.

This way of telling time could be used on cloudy days and at night, but there were troubles, too. The water would freeze on winter nights in a cold climate, and the clock-tender might not mind his work or even fall asleep.

Water clocks did not answer the question *when* but *how long*. A sundial would show that it was noon when the sun was directly overhead; the water clock told only how many hours had passed since the bowl was placed in the water.

Later another much more complicated water clock also had two containers. The water was kept at a certain level in the top container and dripped into the lower container. Here a float, topped with a geared stick, was placed. As

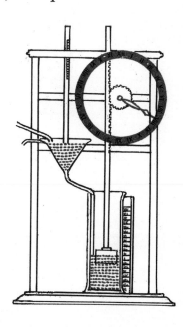

A Water-Clock
Arabic manuscript, early 13th century

the water rose, the float rose. The geared teeth on the stick would fit into the geared teeth on a wheel to which a pointer was fastened. As the wheel turned, the pointer turned to point to the hour on a dial. This was the first time-telling device that looked anything like our modern clocks.

Because the parts had to be made by hand, these water clocks were expensive. Clever craftsmen made them even more so with jewels and decorations. The constant drip, drip, drip of the water could be made to turn trains of cogged wheels which could be made to move small figures, in an amazing manner. This type of water clock was considered a luxury, a gift for kings. Many fine ones are said to have been made in Arabia. The story is told that a Moslem ruler greatly pleased an emperor in Europe by presenting him with the gift of a water clock.

The picture on page 14 shows an Arabic water clock that did many interesting things. The Zodiac was at the top, the doors opened to show men on horseback. At the hour, the birds dropped metal balls into the cups. The musicians also played on their instruments.

One water clock was thought to be enough for each town. It was usually placed in the market place or the public square. Here the wealthy people would send their servants to find out the time. The clock-tender or guard sometimes blew a horn to inform the others.

Water clocks were used in Europe after mechanical clocks were made.

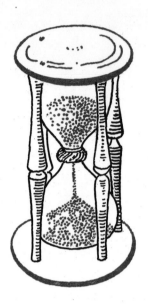

THE SANDGLASS

The sandglass was also useful for telling time. No one knows who invented it or how old it is, but it seems to have developed from the water clock, with sand used in place of water. It was probably first used in lands where water was scarce and there was plenty of sand. A picture of a sandglass found in Rome shows that it was used three hundred years before the birth of Christ.

The sandglass was made of glass either molded or blown. There were two parts with a thin neck in between. In the neck was a tiny hole. The upper part was filled with sand. It took a certain length of time for the sand to run through the hole from the upper part to the lower part. The time might be an hour, a half-hour, or an hour and one half.

The sandglass could be used on cloudy as well as sunny days. It could be used day or night, indoors or outdoors.

16

Sixteenth
Century
ship

Sand did not freeze or evaporate as water does. It ran at an even rate of speed, and a fresh supply was never needed. But the sandglass showed only the passing of a short time, and the glass had to be turned each time all the sand passed through.

Sandglasses were used on ships for telling the speed of a vessel. First a log-line was divided by knots a certain distance apart. A sailor would throw the end of the log-line overboard, and then count the knots that slipped through his fingers as the ship moved through the water. During this time he kept his eyes on a sandglass nearby. He would then announce how many knots an hour the ship was traveling. Sailors still measure distance in *knots* as a man on land does in *miles*.

A three-minute sandglass is still used in kitchens to time the boiling of eggs.

A monastery in Spain.
Monks have put bells in tower,
one monk is pulling the bell ropes.

BELL CLOCKS

During a period in Europe called the Dark Ages there was little change in learning, science, or invention. At that time the people were poor. They worked hard to make a living. The church was an important part of their

18

lives. Some men became monks and lived and studied in monasteries. Here the day was divided into periods for prayer, work, and meals. The sound of a bell told the monks when it was time to change from one occupation to another.

The people who lived in the country around the monasteries began to listen for the sound of the bell to tell time in their own lives.

The bellringer at the church or monastery pulled the bell ropes early in the day for matins or morning prayer. The sound of this bell told the people it was time to get up. The bells were rung twice during the morning and then at noon when it was time to eat the midday meal. The Angelus bell for evening prayer marked the close of the working day—and everyone was glad to hear it.

The word clock came from the French word *cloche* meaning *bell*, or from the Latin *clocka*.

Tower bells, tenth century

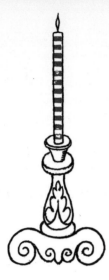

THE CANDLE CLOCK

It is said that King Alfred of England used candles as time-tellers in the 9th Century A.D. King Alfred was a religious man. He declared that he would give one-third of his day to religion. He would give another third of his time to the affairs of his kingdom, and the final third to resting and enjoying himself.

King Alfred noticed that a good candle seemed to burn at an even rate of speed if it were kept out of the wind. He had six 12-inch candles made. Each candle was divided into twelve parts by bands of black and white. Each band would burn for about twenty minutes.

These candles measured a day of twenty-four hours. Three candles were burned during the night. To say it was "two candles" meant that two thirds of the night had passed.

But the candles were not always exactly the same size. They did not really tell the time. They told only how long the candle had been burning.

TOWER CLOCKS

People in Europe gradually became more prosperous. More people moved into cities. They wanted to buy more luxuries. Merchants sent out caravans and ships in search of goods to supply the need.

Some of the travelers visited Arabia. They returned with the news that the Moslems knew a great deal about astronomy and mathematics. They were interested in science, and they were telling time by large weight-driven clocks placed in towers. A heavy weight was tied on the end of a sturdy rope, and the rest of the rope wound around a rod or drum. The weight pulled downward to set the geared wheels of the clock in motion.

Soon tower clocks began to appear in the larger cities of Europe. Most large cities had at least one tower clock. At first the time was struck on a bell by two small figures called "jacks." Many people at that time could not read the numbers on the dial so the bell was needed. At first the dial of a clock had only the hour hand. Later the minute hand was added.

"Jacks"
of Notre-Dame at Dijon,
fourteenth century

The most famous of the early tower clocks was the one in the Cathedral at Strasbourg in Alsace. The clock is a copy of the cathedral. It is three stories high with three dials. One tells the time of day. Another dial tells the day, week, and month. The third dial shows the positions of the planets in the sky. Each day at noon the Twelve Apostles pass in parade, and the Three Wise Men bow before the Christ Child and his Mother. A cock perched on top of one of the towers flaps his wings and crows, "Cock-a-doodle-do! Cock-a-doodle-do!"

People travel for miles to see this unusual clock. Both children and grown-ups like to watch the figures move about.

In 1364 the King of France asked Henry de Vieck, a clockmaker of Württemberg, to build a tower clock for the royal palace. The clockmaker went to work and presented the clock to the king—several years later! But Henry de Vieck made a good clock somewhat like our clocks of today. It was still keeping time after five hundred years.

23

First mechanical cock
Strasbourg clock 1354

Lamp in Cathedral at Pisa

THE PENDULUM

The toothed wheels of the tower clock were handmade, of iron. They were very heavy, and heavy weights were needed to set them in motion. Even de Vieck's clock was not really accurate, but its mechanism was not improved for nearly 300 years.

One day in 1581 a young medical student stood in a church in Pisa, Italy. His name was Galileo. He noticed a lamp hanging by a chain from the ceiling. Something had set the lamp swinging from side to side. At first the lamp swung in a wide arc. Then the distance became shorter and shorter. Galileo observed something that no one had noticed before. The long swing of the lamp seemed to take the same length of time as the shorter swing. Galileo proved this to himself by counting his own heartbeats as the lamp swung back and forth.

24

Huygens' clock mechanism

Later in life Galileo suggested to his son that a pendulum might be used as a regulator on a clock. But Galileo did not actually build the clock.

Between 1640 and 1680 many European clock makers tried to use the pendulum in their clocks. Among these was Christian Huygens, a scientist of Holland, who experimented a great deal with clocks. He combined Galileo's idea with his own and built a satisfactory clock with a pendulum to regulate the mechanism. This clock was so accurate a minute hand was added.

Other clock builders were so impressed they rebuilt their old clocks to use the pendulum as a regulator.

Pendulum clocks had to stand on the floor or hang on the wall so that the balance of the pendulum would not be disturbed. The clock makers sometimes enclosed the working parts, the weight, and the pendulum in an ornamental case of wood. Some of these tall clocks were known as grandfather clocks.

Model of Galileo's clock mechanism, built later

English
spring-driven clock
about 1590

SPRING-DRIVEN CLOCKS

In about 1500 Peter Henlein of Nuremberg, Germany, found that he could use a spring instead of a weight as the driving power in clocks. He used a long thin ribbon of steel called a *mainspring*. One end was fastened to the winding arbor and the spring was wound up tight. As the spring unwound, it pressed against the clock's toothed wheels to set them in motion. A *balance wheel* instead of a pendulum was used to keep the wheels in the clock mechanism turning at an even rate. A small *hairspring* inside the balance wheel made it turn first in one direction and then in the other.

The use of the mainspring and balance wheel meant that clocks need no longer be designed with weights and

26

Elephant clock (1700) moves trunk and ears

pendulum. They no longer needed to hang on the wall or stand on the floor. The spring-driven clock could be made in a smaller, compact form that could be placed on a table or shelf.

Clock makers in Germany, France, and England made table clocks. Many of them were cleverly designed and richly decorated. Some were trimmed with jewels. Some even had an alarm bell which could be set to ring at a certain time. All were made by hand, and all were high in price. They were found only in the palaces of the rulers and the homes of rich families.

Some of these early table clocks may be seen in American and European museums today.

27

HOW A MECHANICAL
CLOCK WORKS

Several things must be present in every mechanical clock. There must be *power to make the clock run*. This may be supplied by the downward pull of a weight or the unwinding of a mainspring.

There must be something to *transmit the power* to the hands that point to the numbers on the dial. Toothed wheels do this. One wheel makes a complete turn once every hour carrying the minute hand with it. The wheel which moves the hour hand makes one-twelfth of a turn each hour.

There must be a means of *controlling the power*. In weight-driven clocks the pendulum swing is used to regulate the speed at which the clock wheels run. The speed of the pendulum may be regulated by changing the length or the weight of the pendulum.

28

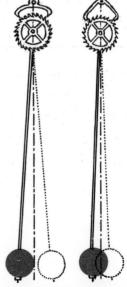

A device called the *escapement* is also important. This is a curved piece of metal with hooks called pallets at the ends. As the escapement tilts from side to side the pallets fit into the teeth of a notched wheel. This controls the speed of the wheels to the speed of the pendulum. It also supplies the pendulum with enough energy to continue swinging.

In spring-driven clocks the balance wheel does the work of the pendulum, and the hairspring regulates the speed of the balance-wheel controlled by the escapement.

There must be something for *making the time known*. The *hands point to the numbers on the dial* to do this.

EARLY WATCHES

The idea of a very small timepiece which might be carried in the pocket may not be traced to any one man. Peter Henlein of Nuremberg is said to have used a mainspring in such a clock. He made the mechanism by hand and placed it in an oval-shaped case of iron. Because of this shape these early watches were sometimes called "Nuremberg eggs."

Later, watches were designed in the shapes of flowers, books, butterflies, stars, cockle shells, and even skulls.

30

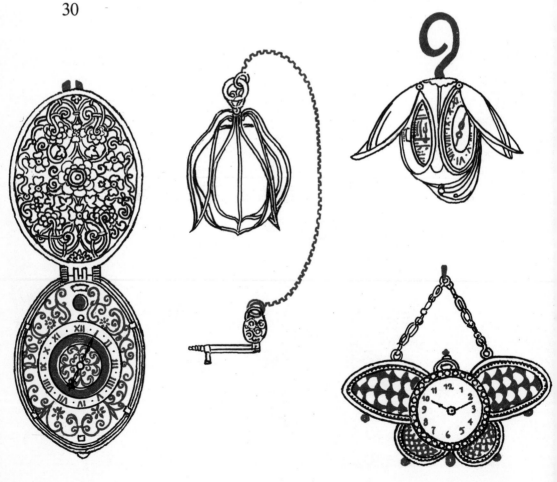

These watches were not accurate timekeepers, but they were very handsome. Made of gold and silver, they were enameled in color and decorated with jewels. They were not carried in the pocket, but worn as a piece of jewelry on a chain, or pinned to the clothing. Early watches, like early clocks, could be bought only by wealthy people. Most people could not afford to buy them.

The art of watchmaking spread through Germany to England, France and Switzerland. The Swiss became famous for their watches.

31

CLOCKMAKING IN AMERICA

In the early days a few clockmakers came to America from England and Holland. They brought the tools of their trade with them. They made clocks by hand one at a time to please each purchaser. At this time clocks were made that could be hung on the wall. A clock of this kind was called a wag-on-the-wall.

Later clockmakers learned their trade in this country. Among these was Eli Terry, fourteen years old. In 1786 he began to learn the clock trade under Thomas Harland, a clockmaker who had come from England to open up a shop in Connecticut.

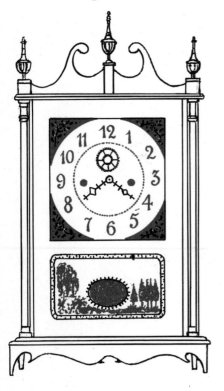

By the time he was twenty-one Eli had completed his first clock. It was a grandfather clock with weight and pendulum in a handsome case.

Then Eli Terry opened a shop of his own. Around 1800 he got the idea that he could use water power in his shop—the water to come from "Niagra Brook" across the street. Later he was joined by Seth Thomas and Silas Hoadley, and the three decided to make five hundred clocks at a time. This was a large undertaking in those days.

32

Eli Terry
selling works for clocks

Eli Terry rode through the countryside on a horse peddling the clocks they had made. Usually only the works of the clocks dangled from Eli's saddle—the people who bought them would have a local carpenter make a case for the clock. The clocks were made of wood and sold for four dollars each.

Eli Terry was somewhat of an inventor. He designed a weight and pendulum clock that was much smaller than the grandfather clock. It could be placed on a shelf. In 1814 Eli Terry had this clock patented. The clock was made by the hundreds of thousands and made Eli Terry rich. It is shown on page 32.

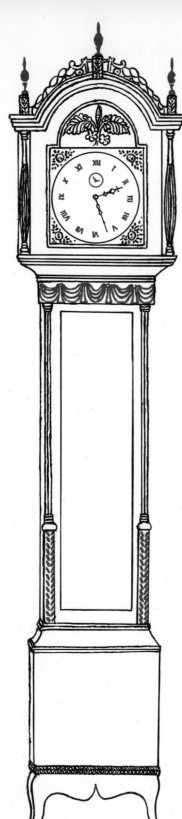

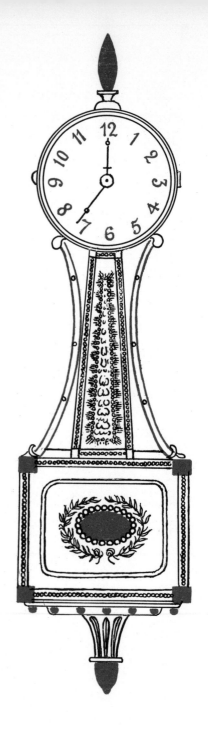

Grandfather clock

Seth Thomas bought the right to make Eli Terry's patented clock for a thousand dollars. He opened a clock factory of his own and it, too, prospered. Seth Thomas clocks were sold all over the world, and there is a clock company with this name today.

Most of these early clocks were made with wood parts. It was hard to get the proper woods for the wheels and plates, and the wood had to be seasoned for a year before it was carved. Brass parts were used in some expensive eight-day clocks.

A clockmaker named Chauncey Jerome had worked with Eli Terry. One night in 1837 he had the idea that he could make an inexpensive one-day brass clock that would take the place of the wood clock. This clock was successful from the start.

Another famous American clock was the Banjo Clock designed by Simon Willard of Massachusetts. This was a handsome clock that looked like a banjo in shape. The clocks were weight-driven, with pendulum, and had eight-day movements made of brass. The cases combined mahogany, gilded wood, and painted glass. There was usually a brass ornament at the top.

All these men lived in the New England states, and these states became famous for clockmaking. Connecticut was the most famous of all. Today many clocks are still made there.

The Ingersoll watch

WATCHES IN AMERICA

Watches were not made in America as early as clocks. A few were made for special customers. About 1850 Edward Howard and Aaron L. Dennison set up a small watch factory which later became the great Waltham Company.

One of the first successful American watches was the Waterbury watch. There were many jokes about this watch because it took so long to wind it—its mainspring was nine feet long!

Another famous American watch was an inexpensive one made by the R. H. Ingersoll Company. This time-keeper was really more like a little alarm clock than a watch, but it could be carried in one's pocket. It cost a

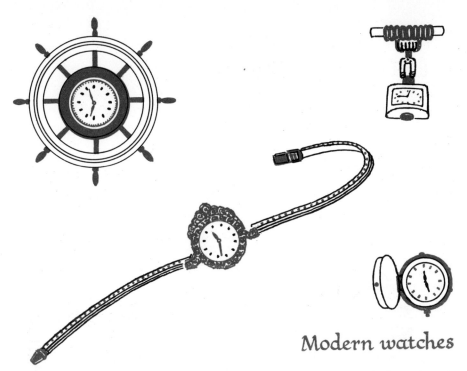

Modern watches

dollar and was advertised with the slogan, "The watch that made the dollar famous."

Today many kinds of watches are made in American factories. Some are set in bracelets and worn as wrist-watches. Others are small enough to be worn as rings. Some watches are operated by a tiny electric battery the size of a small button. Some modern watches are self-winding. The mainspring of such a watch winds itself as it is worn.

Some watches are shock-proof and water-proof. Some have dials with hands and numbers in luminous material so that they may be seen in the dark.

Some watches are made with second hands so that doctors and nurses may easily count how many times a patient's heart beats in one minute.

ELECTRIC CLOCKS

Today many homes, schools, and public buildings have electric clocks. An electric clock looks like a mechanical clock, but has a cord that leads to an electric outlet. The electric clock has no pendulum—its regulator isn't even inside the clock! The electric clock is regulated by the alternating current that comes from an electric power plant. This controls the motor that moves the hands on the dial.

Such electric clocks keep time with great accuracy—if the cord is not disconnected from the outlet, or the flow of current stopped by a storm.

Some portable and wall clocks today are powered by flashlight batteries or by transistors. These electric clocks require no cords, and they are extremely reliable.

Some electric clocks have an alarm which may be set to ring at a certain time. Others are built in the same case with a radio. These clocks may be set to turn on the radio at a certain time.

Even modern clocks do not always tell the exact time. Some clocks are said to be "fast." Others are "slow."

Clocks in the United States are set from a master clock in the Naval Observatory Building at Georgetown, near Washington, D.C. From here signals giving the time are sent out over telegraph wires and naval radio stations.

The Naval Observatory Building is a sturdy building with very thick walls. The master clock is placed in a glass-enclosed, air-tight, dustproof chamber. The floor of this room is concrete eight inches thick so that nothing may jar the clock.

In the Naval Observatory there are special telescopes called Photographic Zenith Tubes. These are used to photograph the stars.

Four photographs are taken of a certain star—two just before the star passes the center hairline on the lens, and two just after. The time of each photograph is electrically recorded, and the clock is checked by experts. If the clock agrees with the stars, it is correct, or very nearly so.

39

SOME FAMOUS CLOCKS

Thousands of clocks and watches were made through the years by hundreds of skilled craftsmen. Some have become famous because of their size, beauty, or unusual features.

The most famous clock in England is the Westminster Clock in the Victoria Tower in the houses of Parliament in London. It is often referred to as "Big Ben" though the name really applies to the *bell* of the clock. This bell was so enormous sixteen horses were needed to haul it from the foundry where it was cast to the tower where it was to be installed.

Face of Big Ben

Clock tower in St. Mark's Square

No trip to Italy would be complete without seeing the clock on the clock tower in St. Mark's Square in Venice. Its big dial shows the time with two sets of figures from one to twelve. The dial also shows the motions of the sun and moon and the signs of the Zodiac. At the very top of the tower two giant size bronze figures strike the hours on a bell with their big hammers.

A famous American clock was the one completed in 1880 by Felix Meyer after ten years of labor. This clock was 18 feet high and 8 feet wide with many moving figures. The quarter hour was struck on a bell by a baby, the half hour by a young man, the three quarters by an old man, and the hour by a figure supposed to be death. The figure of George Washington presented a scroll of the Declaration of Independence. Then a door opened and other presidents appeared. They saluted Washington and went back into the clock.

Many unusual clocks may be seen in American and European museums today.

ATOMIC CLOCKS

Through the years man has been trying to make clocks more accurate. Shortly after the American Revolution scientists all over the world became interested in the study of the atom. Some scientists tried to apply their knowledge to clockmaking.

The first atomic clock, known as the Atomichron, was invented by Dr. J. R. Zacharias. This is a complicated machine and does not look like a clock as we think of one. It has no dial and no hands. It is so accurate it will lose only one second in 3000 years.

The first Atomichrons manufactured* cost about fifty thousand dollars. They were seven feet tall and weighed about six hundred pounds. Atomichrons are in use at the U.S. Bureau of Standards at Washington, D. C. and at Boulder, Colorado. They are also used in a few research laboratories.

Atomic clocks are not designed for general use. They will be used by scientists who need to measure time exactly.

They will probably be used to keep television and radio stations on the right frequency. They may be used on ships, submarines, and aircraft.

An Atomichron for space rockets is now being prepared. This one will weigh only sixty-five pounds. It will take up a little less than a cubic foot of space in the rocket.

*By the National Company, Inc. of Malden, Mass.

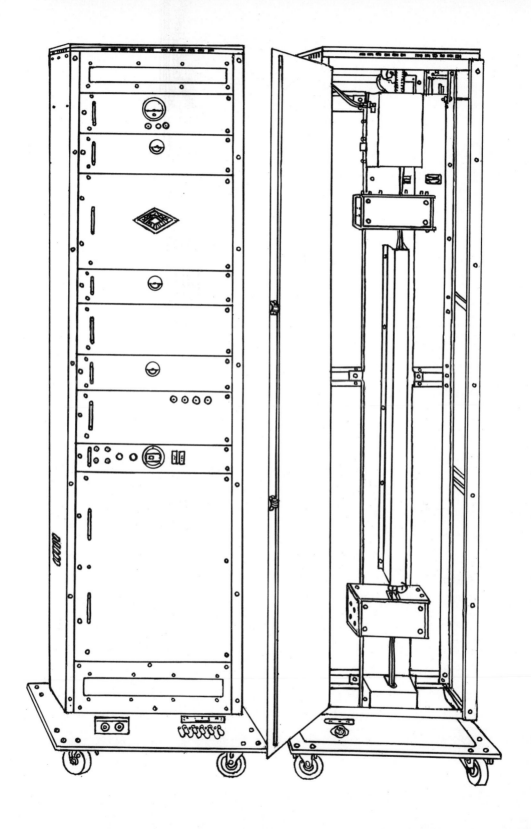

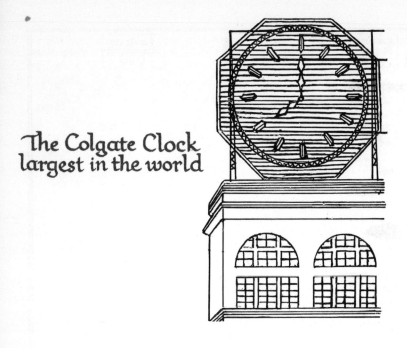

The Colgate Clock
largest in the world

TIME ZONES
IN THE UNITED STATES

It is eight o'clock in the morning, and in New York City thousands of people are hurrying to work. Many of them glance at the Colgate clock which faces New York harbor. This is the largest clock in the world. Its dial is fifty feet wide, and its hands weigh over two thousand pounds.

But eight o'clock in New York City is not eight o'clock in other parts of the country. In this country people living along the Atlantic Ocean are first to see daylight. As the earth turns, the people in the middle states are next to receive light from the sun. The people living along the Pacific Coast are the last to see the sun in the morning.

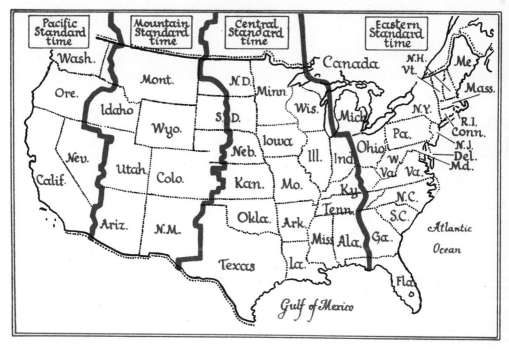

In pioneer days when travel was slow, this difference in time did not seem to matter. But when the railroads were built coast to coast, and the speed of travel increased, time had to be measured more exactly.

In 1883 a meeting called by the railroads divided the United States into four Standard Time Zones. The states along the Atlantic Ocean have Eastern Standard Time. The states in the middle west have Central Standard Time. The Rocky Mountain states have Mountain Standard Time, and the states along the Pacific Coast have Pacific Standard Time.

When it is 12 noon in New York City it is 11 o'clock in Chicago. It is 10 o'clock in Denver, Colorado, and it is only 9 o'clock in Los Angeles or San Francisco, California.

In whatever zone you live, the correct time is usually available today. Inside homes and buildings you will see clocks everywhere. If you ride in a car, you will probably see a clock on the dashboard.

You may consult a watch on your wrist, or glance at a tower clock in a tall building. If you are in a city, you will see clocks in shop windows. You may see clocks erected on tall pedestals along the sidewalks.

You may hear the time announced on the radio, or you may ask the time from your telephone company.

Years ago only kings and rulers could know the answer to the question, "What time is it?" Today almost everyone knows!

Clocks tell the time!